Introduction

Infrared Photography: Capturing the Invisible World, unveils the ethereal beauty of a hidden spectrum, taking readers on a journey through hauntingly beautiful gothic cemeteries, majestic architectural marvels, and surreal landscapes. This book combines striking, high-contrast images with insightful commentary on the art and technique of infrared photography.

Explore how ordinary scenes transform into extraordinary visions under the infrared lens, where lush foliage glows eerily white, skies deepen into dramatic shadows, and stone monuments take on an otherworldly texture. Designed for both seasoned photographers and curious beginners, the book provides tips on equipment, shooting techniques, and post-processing to master this captivating form of art.

Whether you're drawn to the quiet solemnity of cemeteries, the timeless allure of gothic architecture, or the dreamlike quality of infrared landscapes, **Infrared Photography: Capturing the Invisible World** will inspire and elevate your photographic journey into the unseen.

Cemeteries

Chapter One

Infrared photography of cemeteries creates a hauntingly beautiful and ethereal aesthetic, transforming ordinary scenes into otherworldly visions. In this genre, foliage appears glowing white or silvery, giving the impression of a winter landscape even in summer. Tombstones and monuments, rendered in high contrast against the bright surroundings, exude a timeless and serene quality. The sky often takes on dramatic dark tones, adding a sense of depth and mystery. These images evoke a blend of tranquility and the supernatural, capturing the spiritual essence of these sacred grounds in a uniquely surreal and artistic manner.

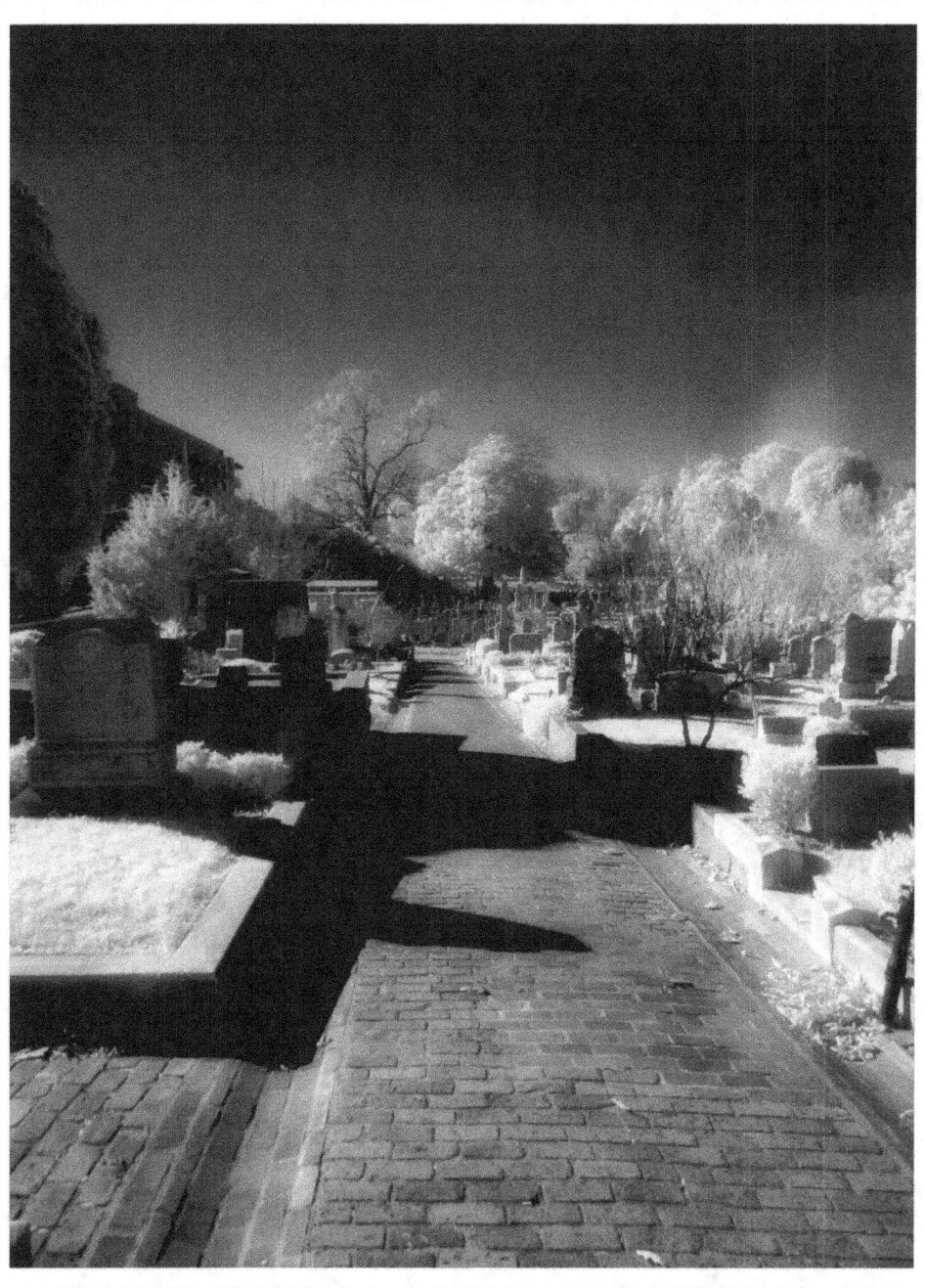

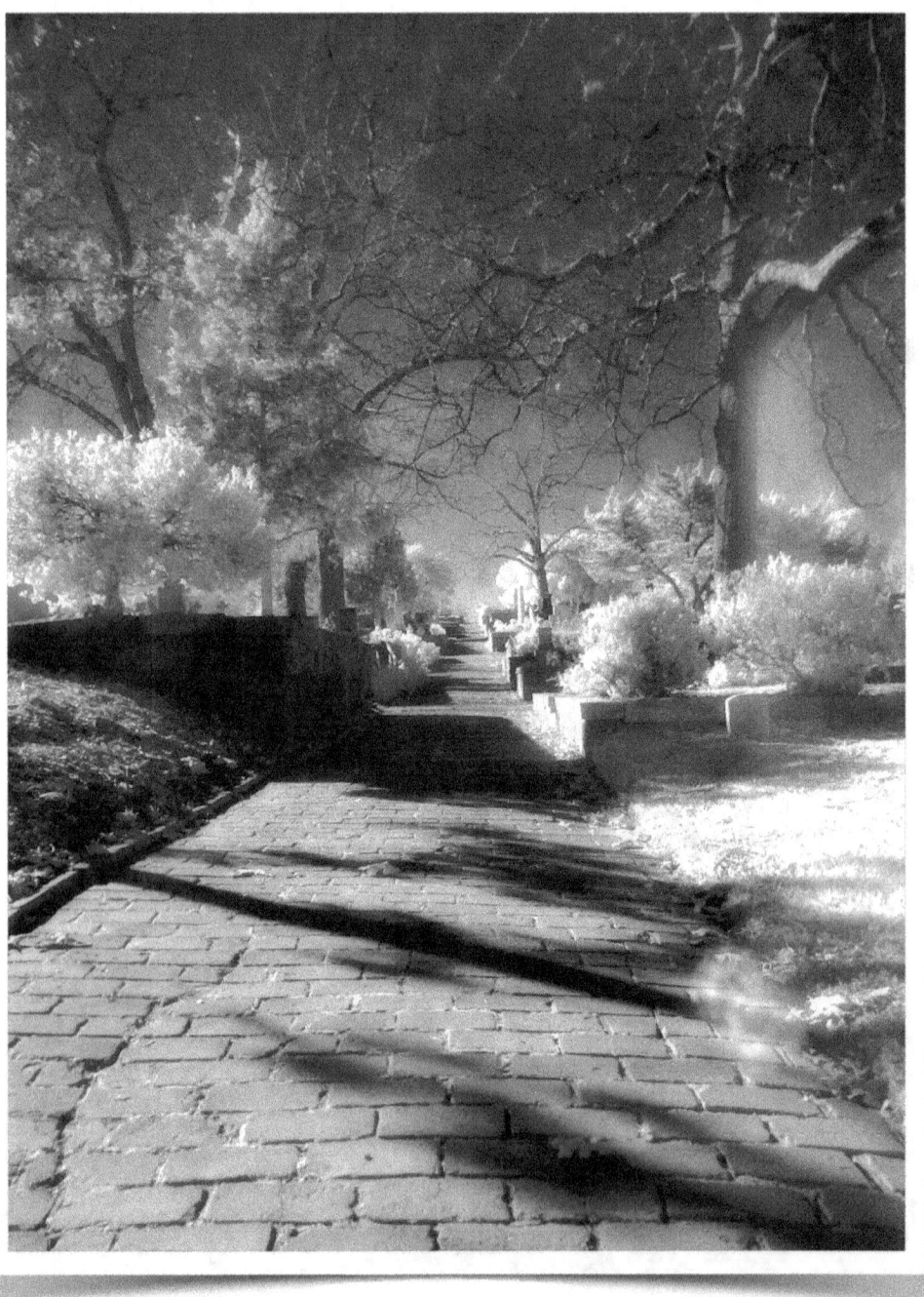

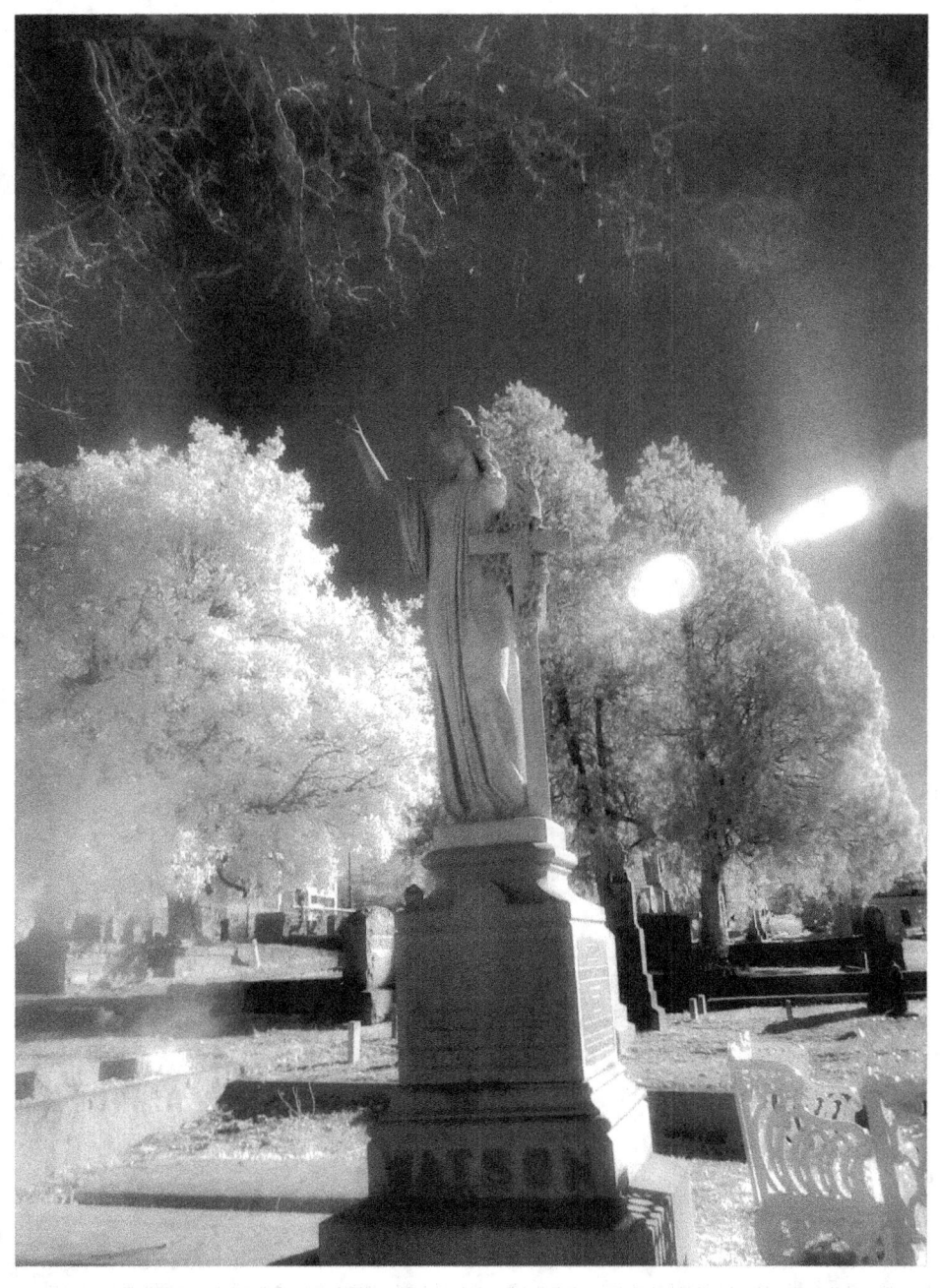

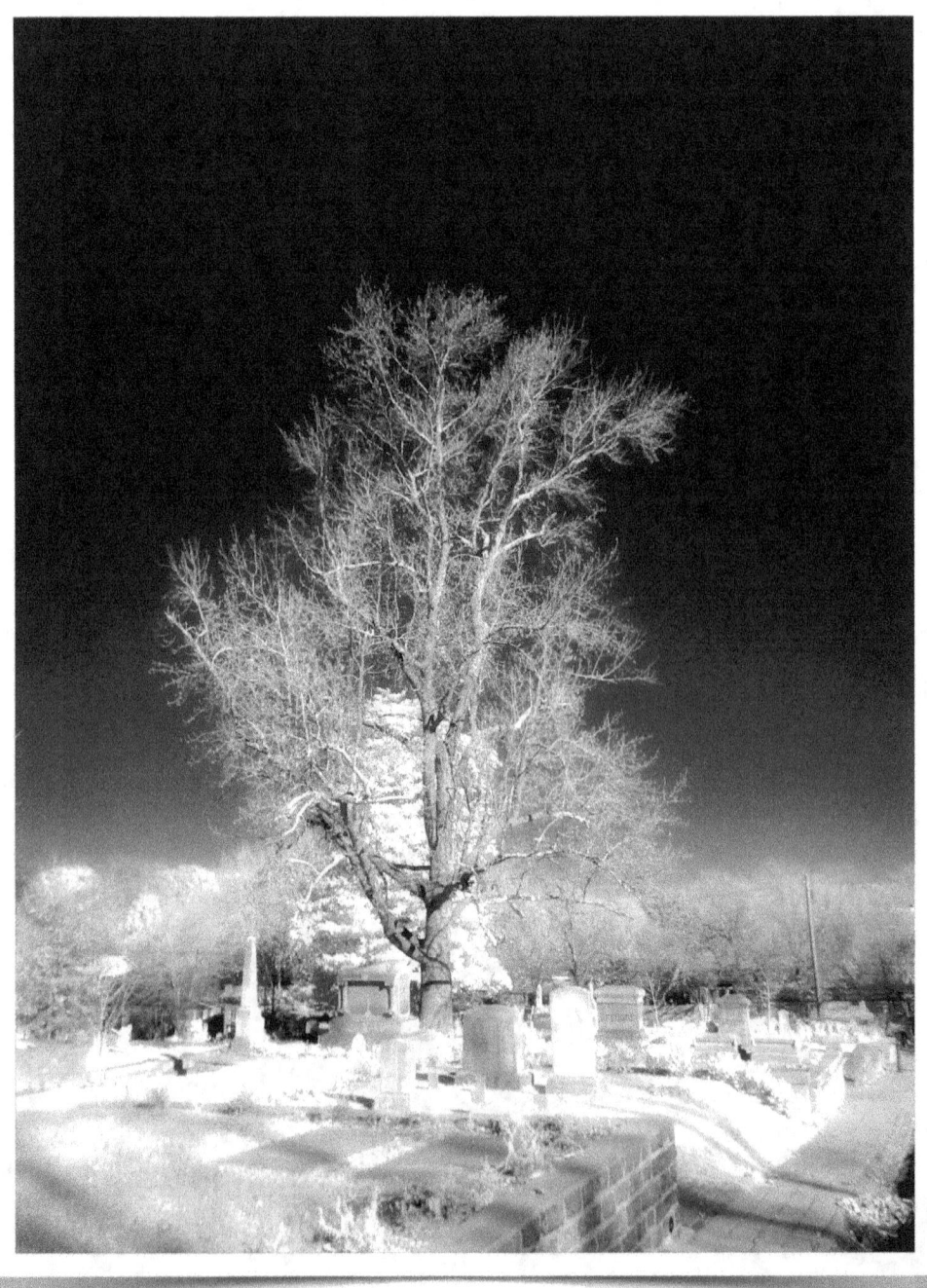

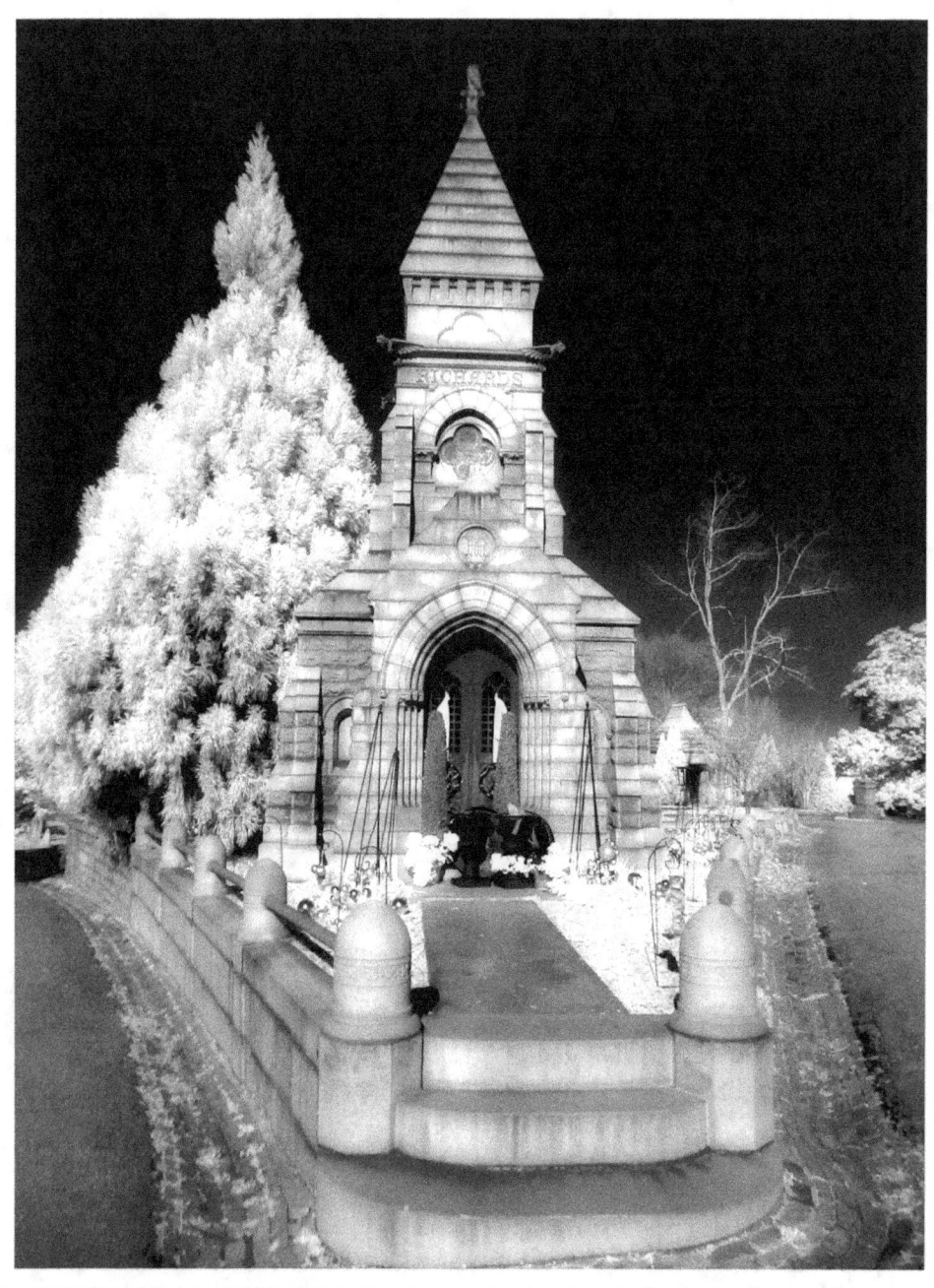

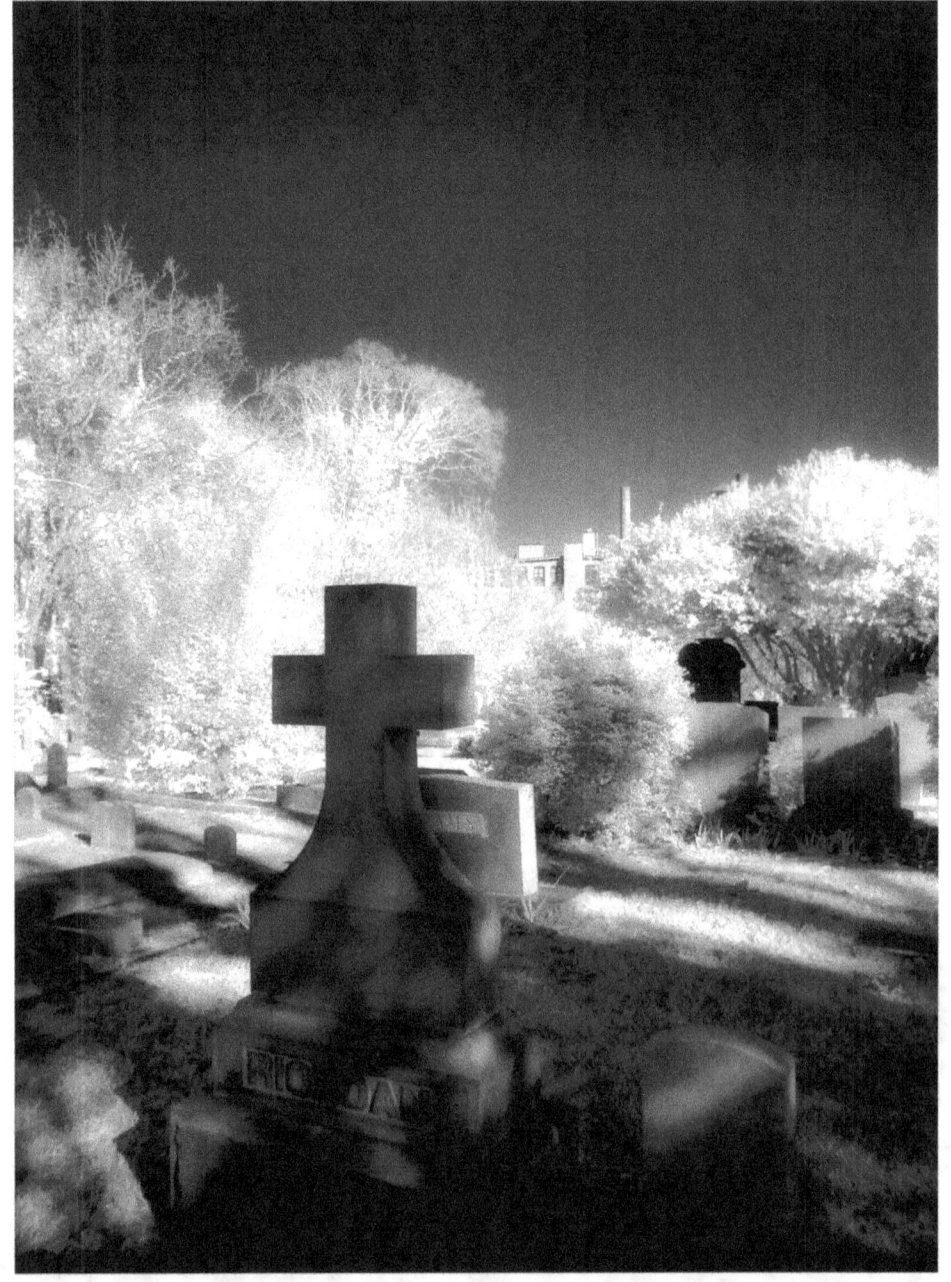

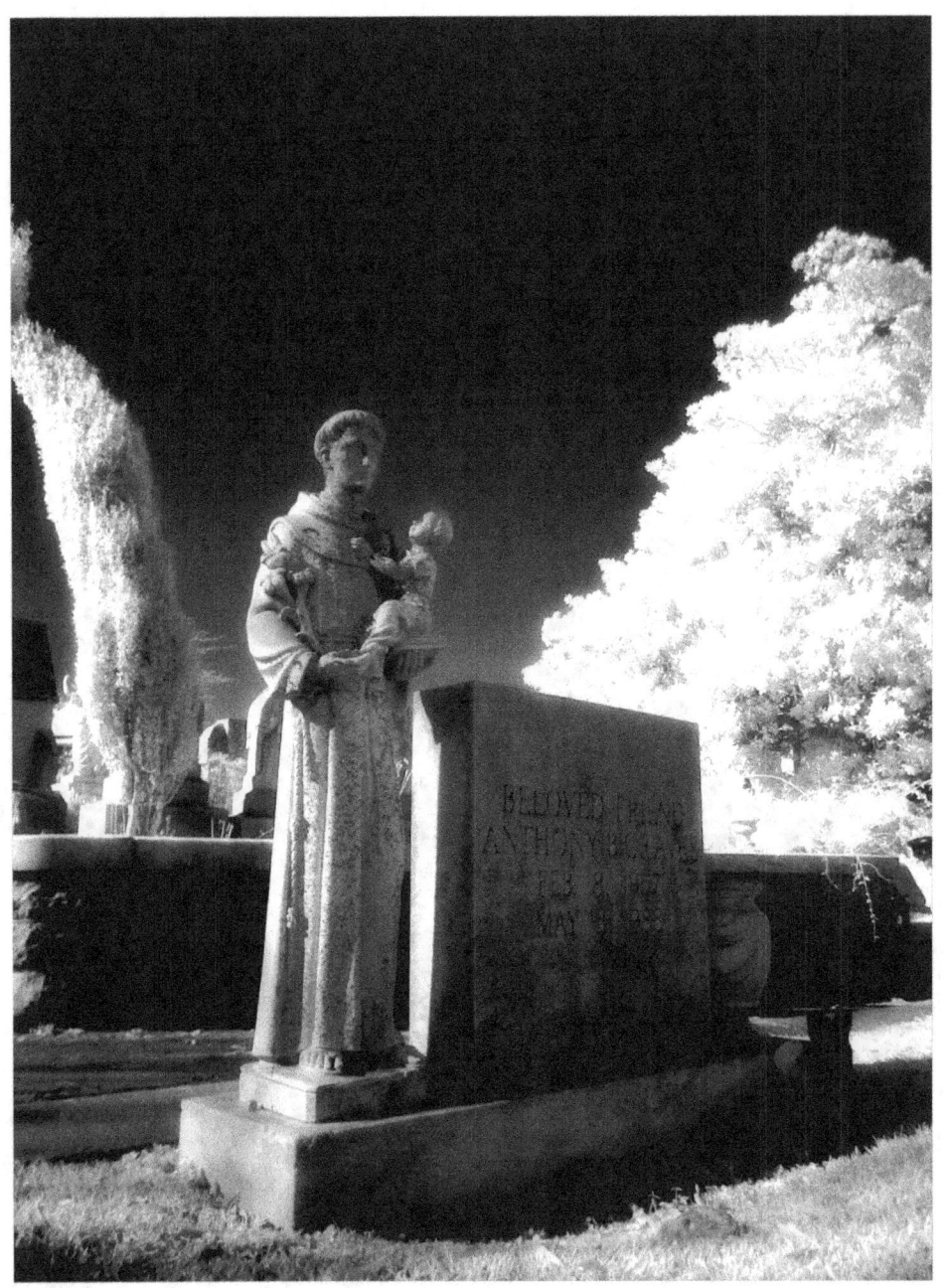

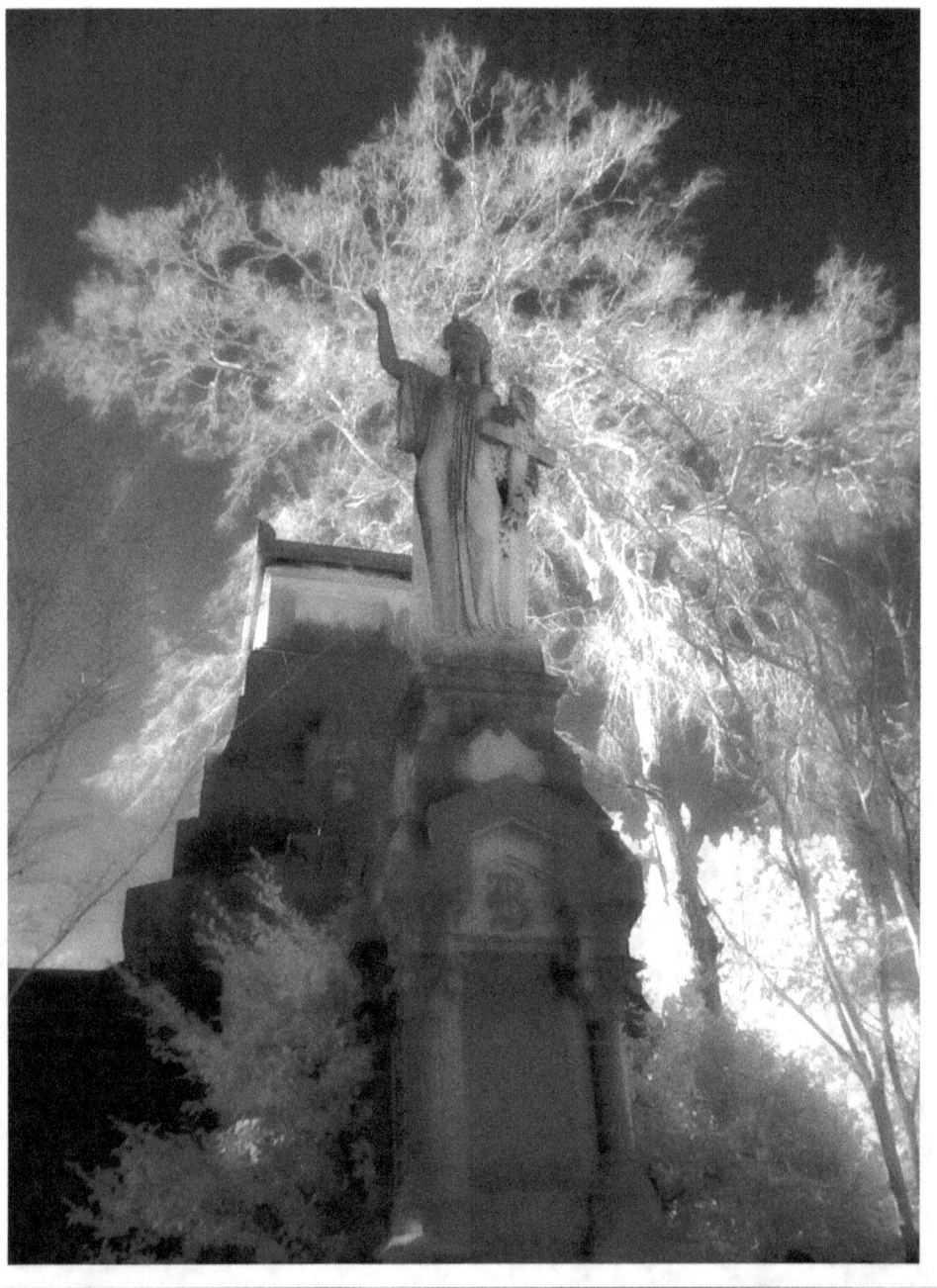

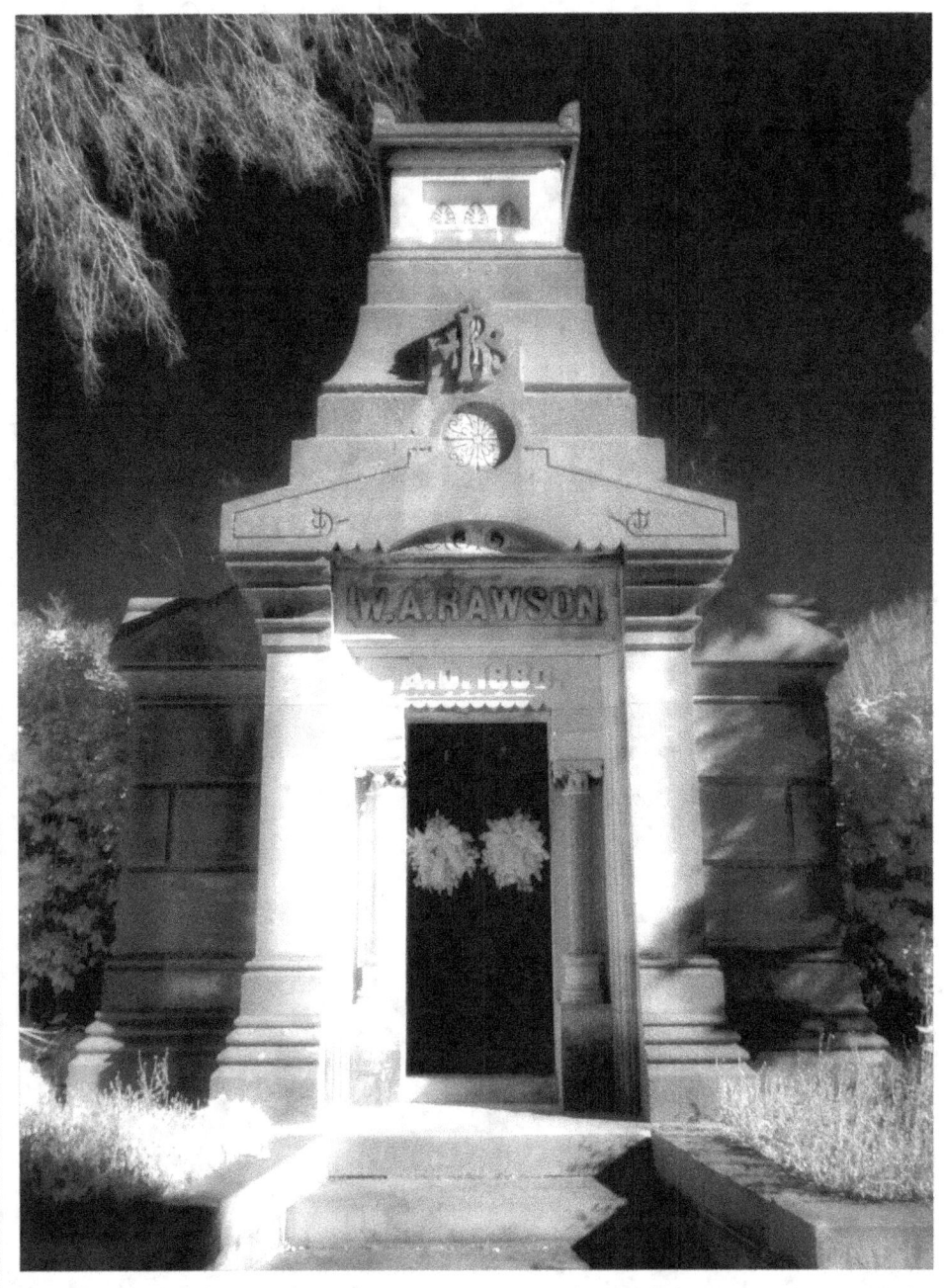

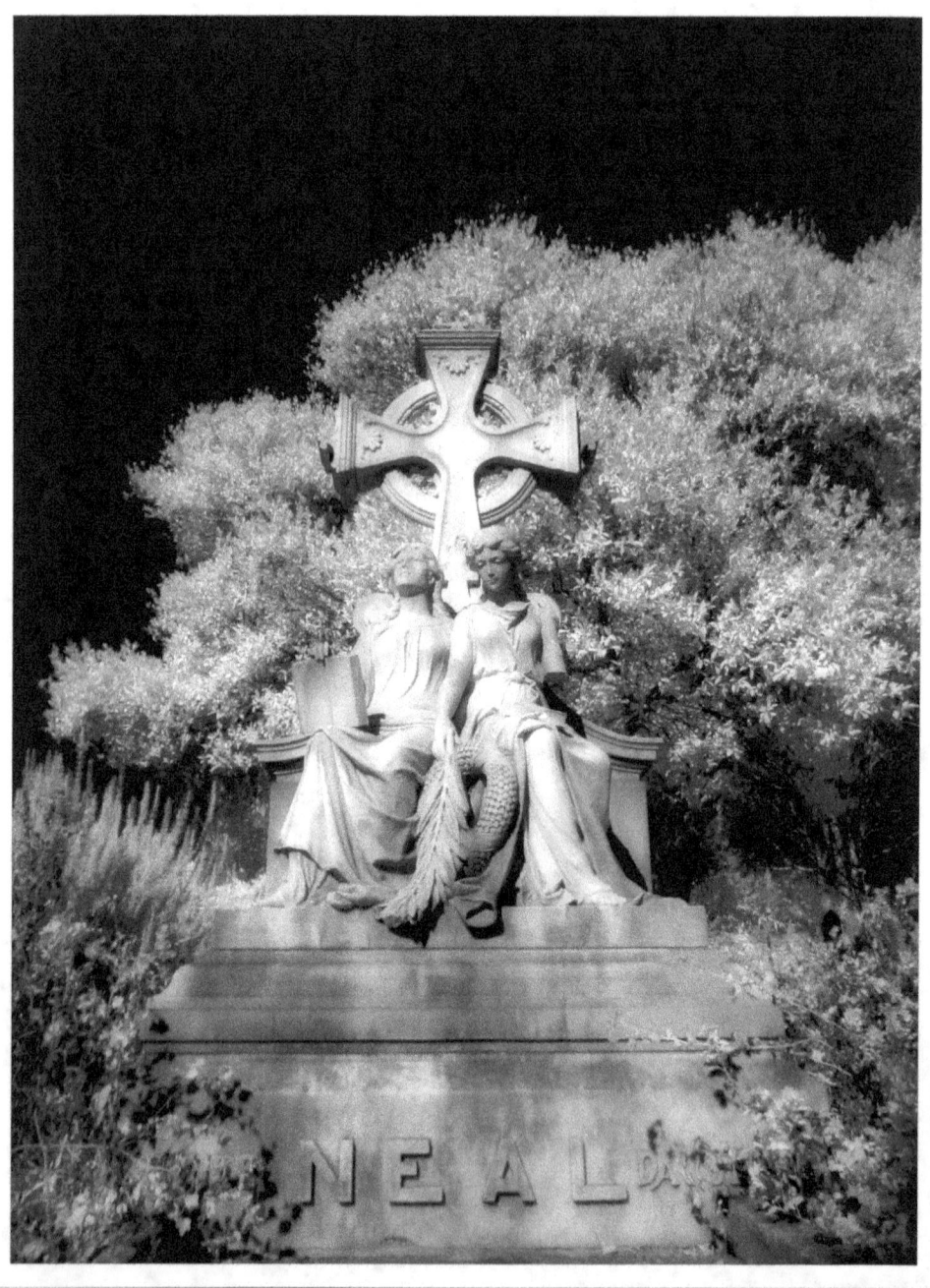

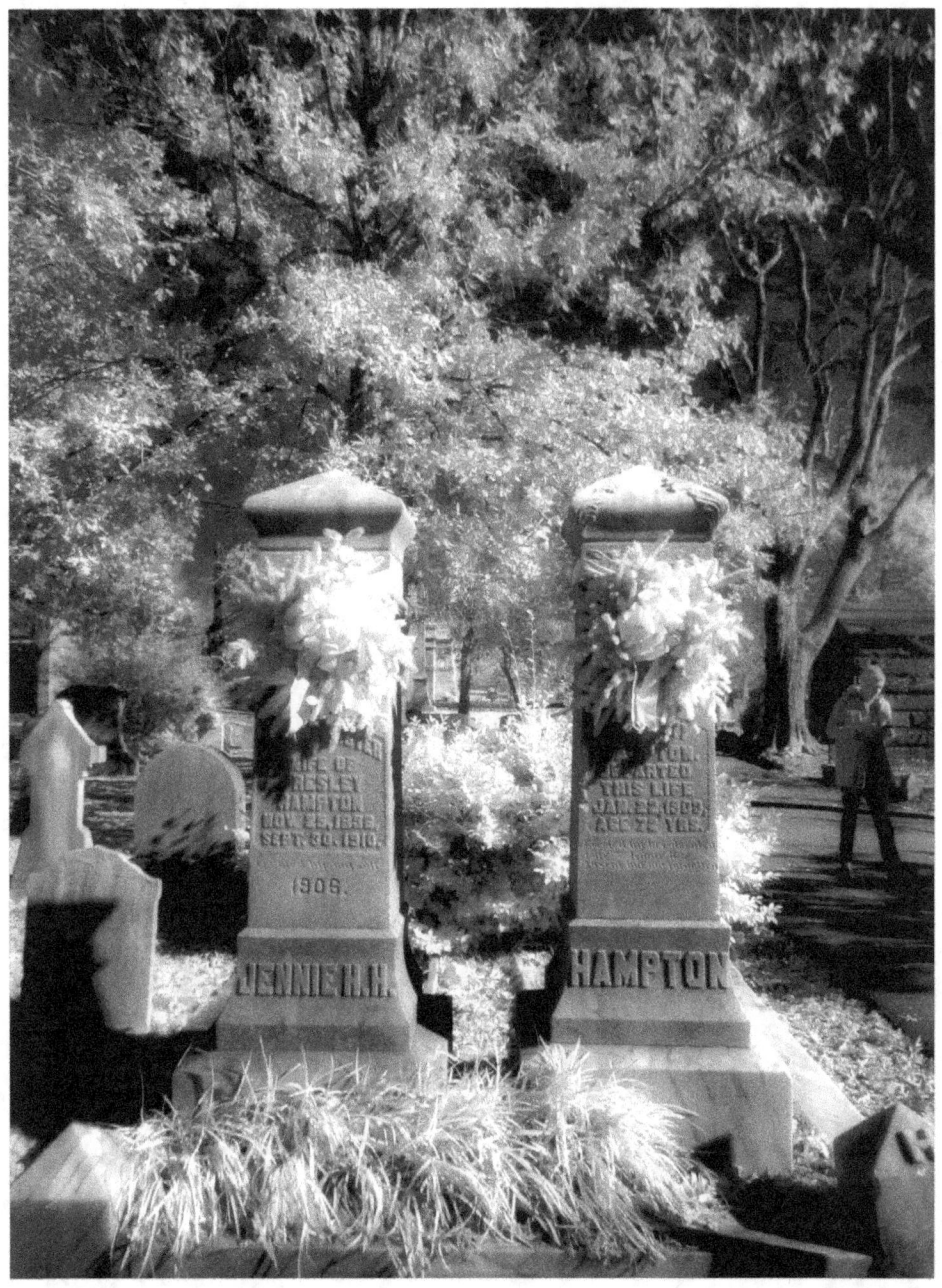

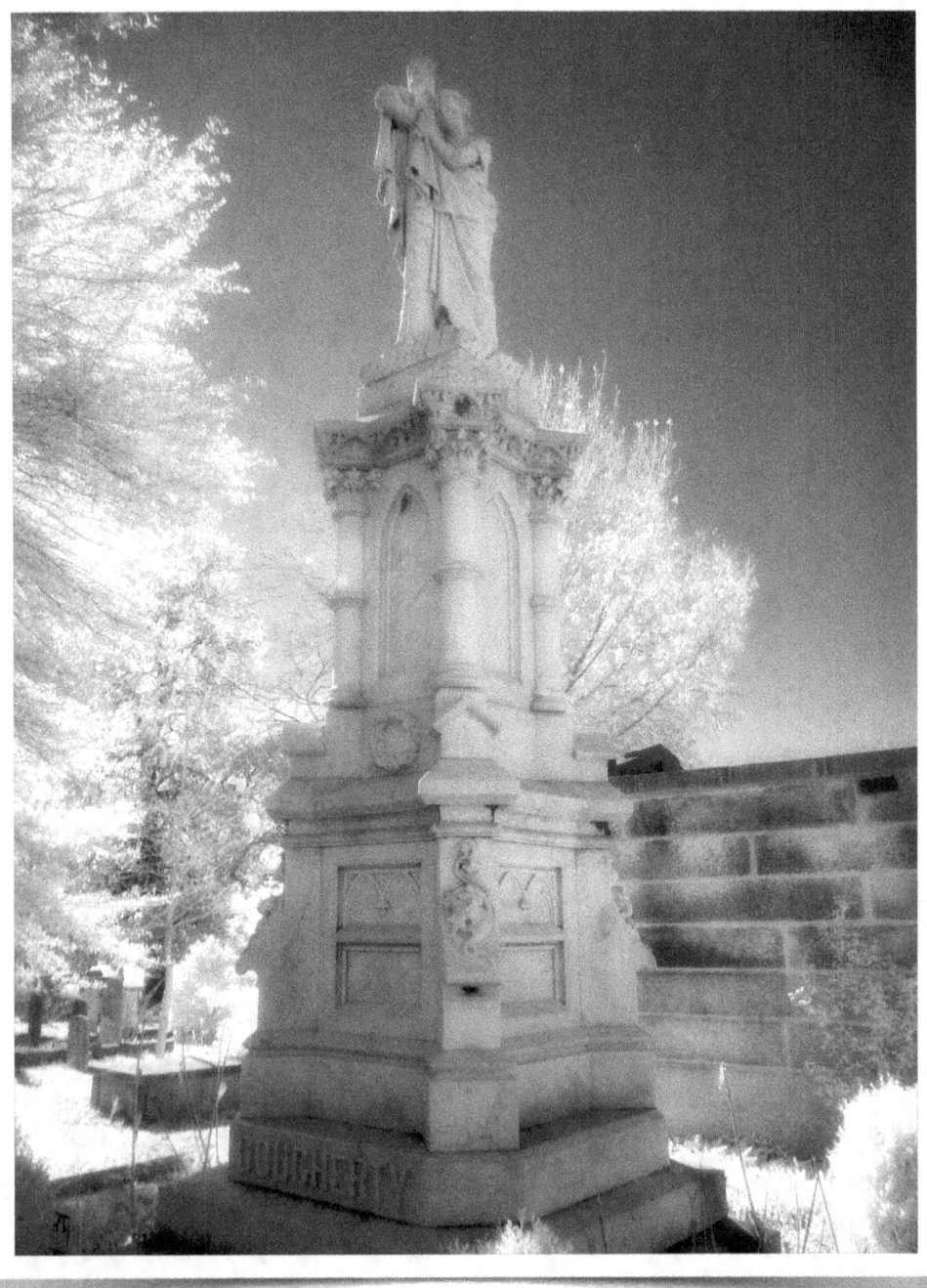

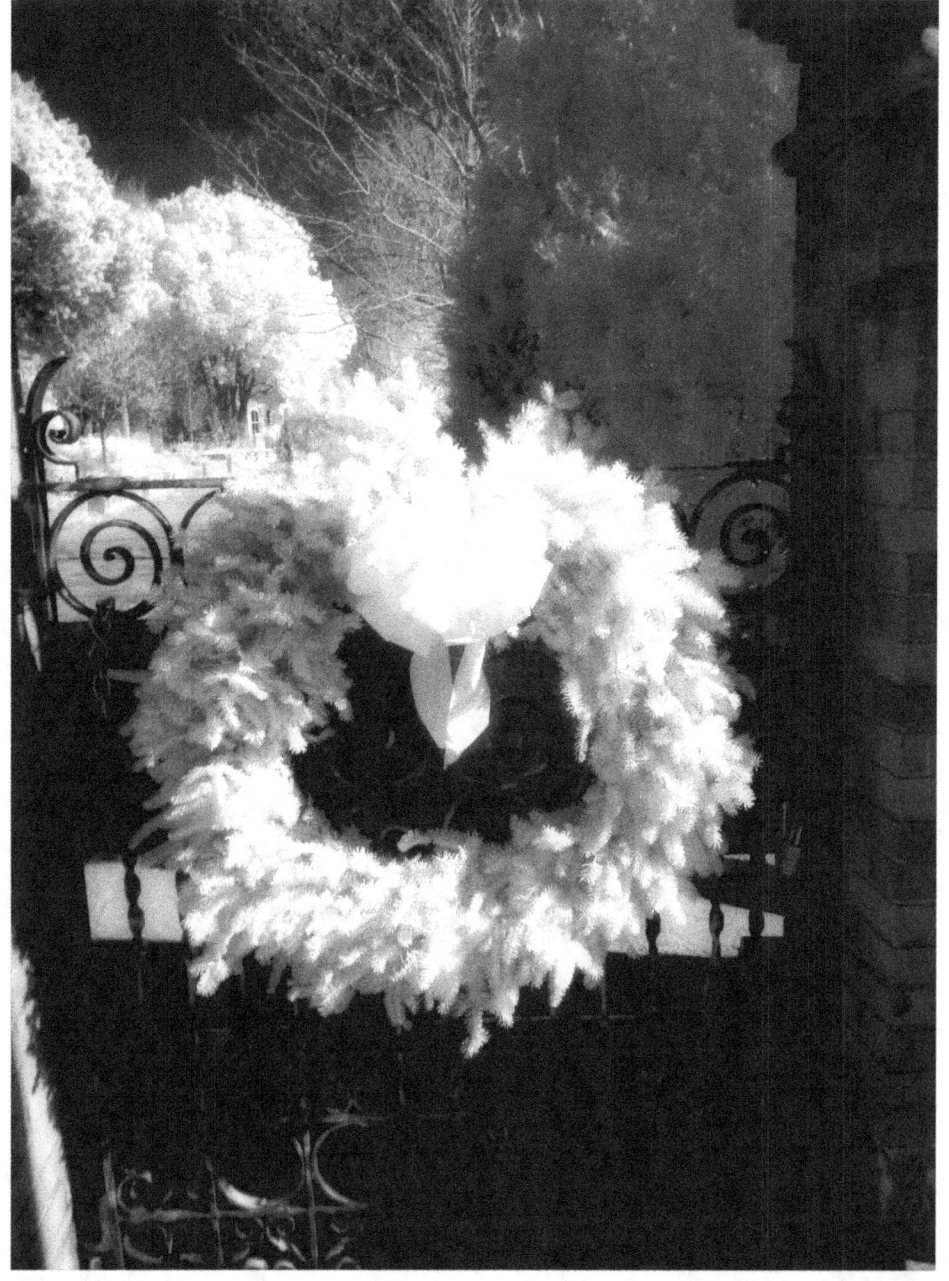

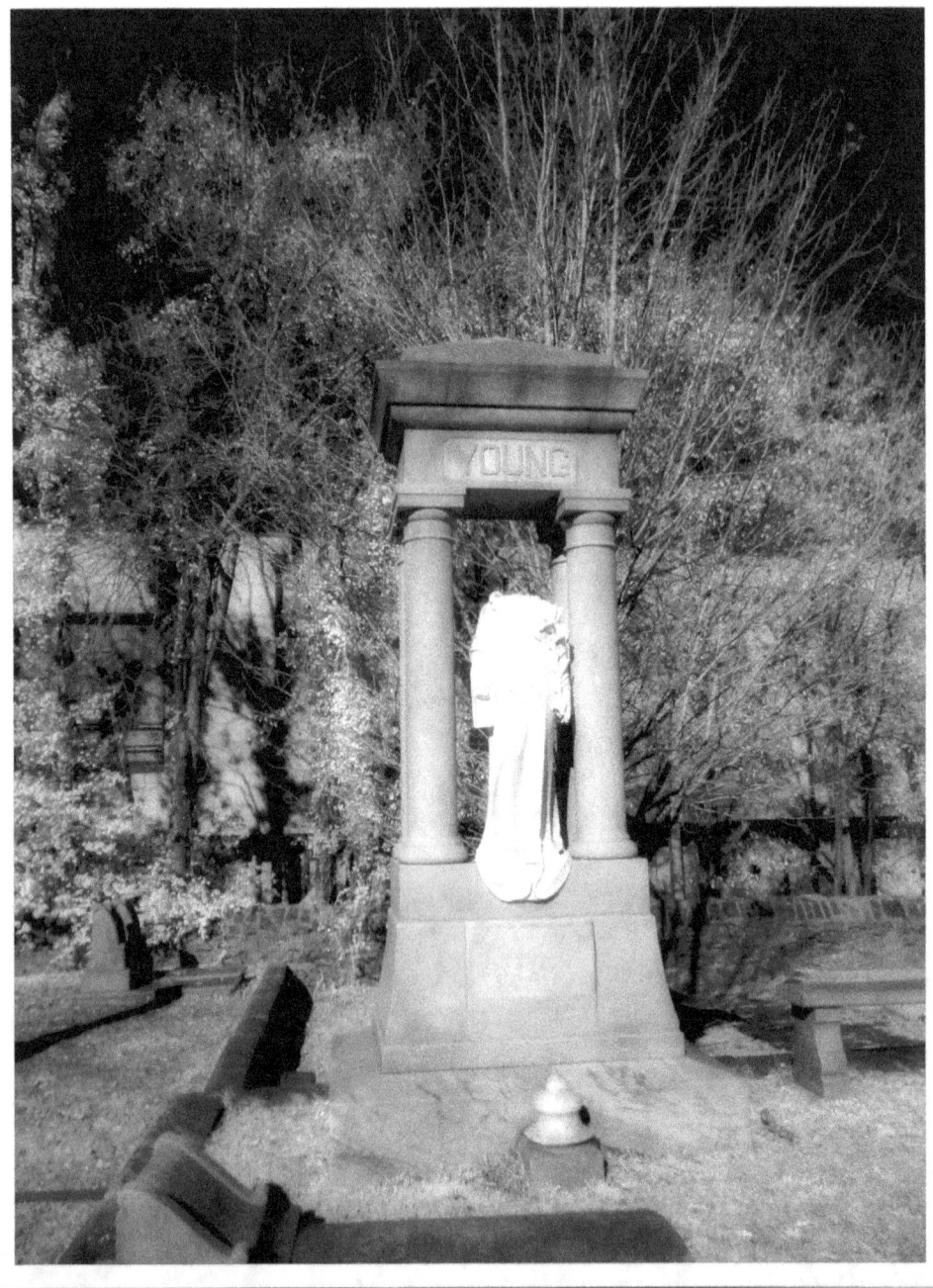

Landscapes

Chapter Two

Infrared photography transforms landscapes into otherworldly scenes by capturing light beyond the visible spectrum, typically between 700nm and 900nm. Vegetation, rich in chlorophyll, reflects infrared light, rendering trees, grass, and foliage in striking whites and silvers, creating a surreal, "snow-like" effect often called the "Wood Effect." Meanwhile, skies deepen to dramatic, inky blacks, and water surfaces take on a smooth, glassy quality. This stark contrast highlights intricate details and textures, producing images with an ethereal and dreamlike aesthetic. Infrared landscapes evoke a sense of mystery and timelessness, offering a fresh and imaginative perspective on the natural world.

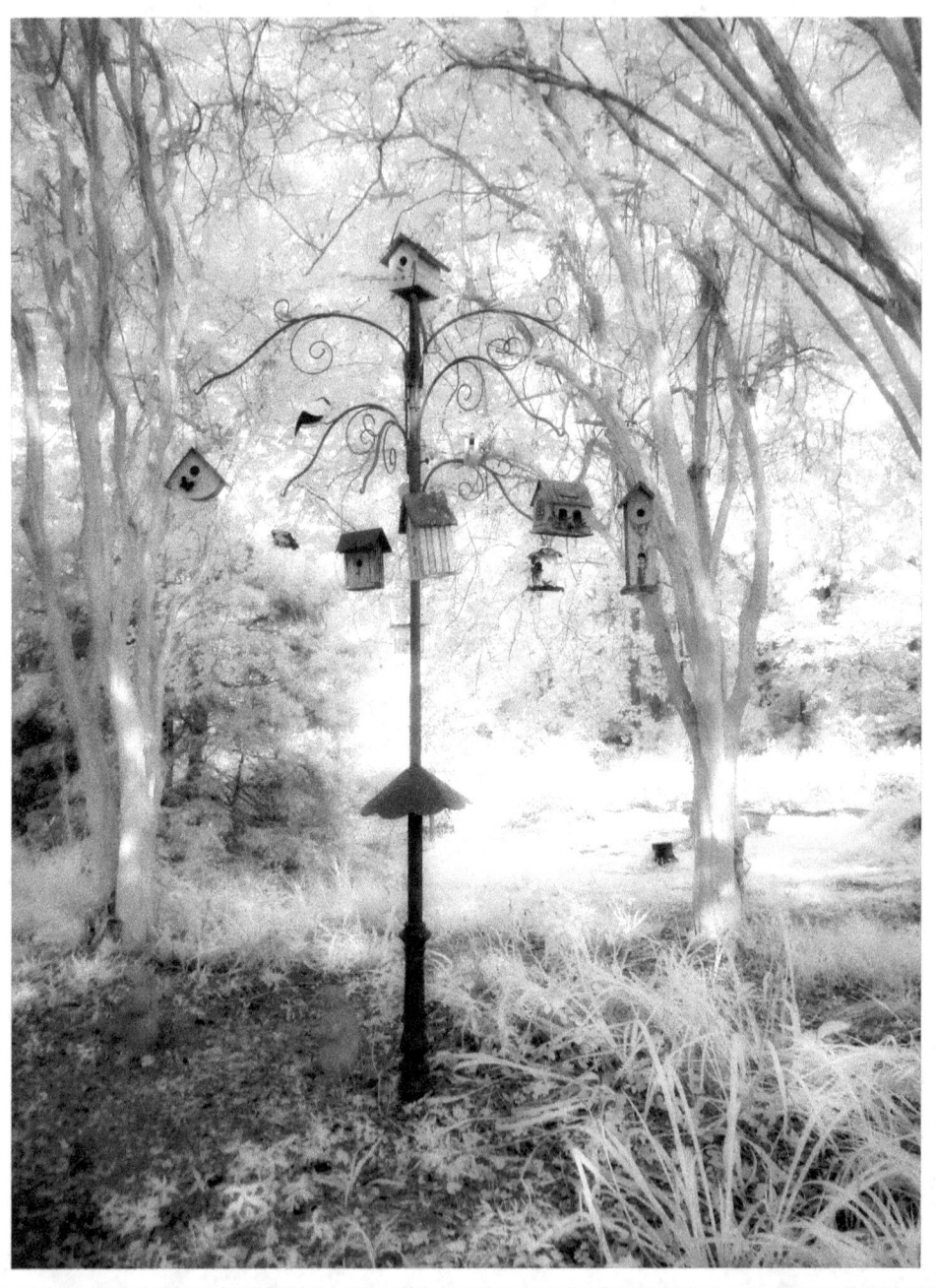

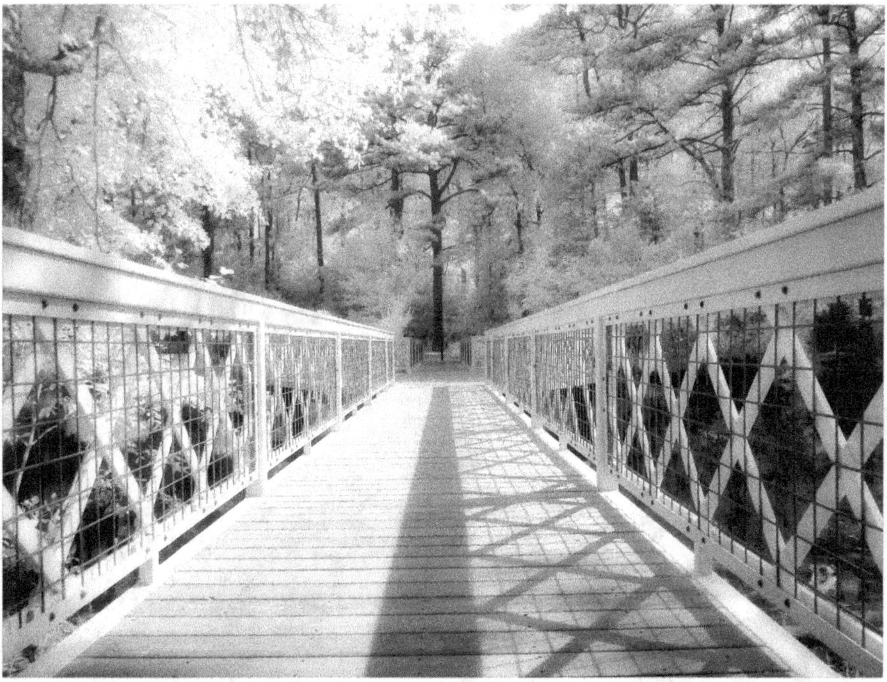

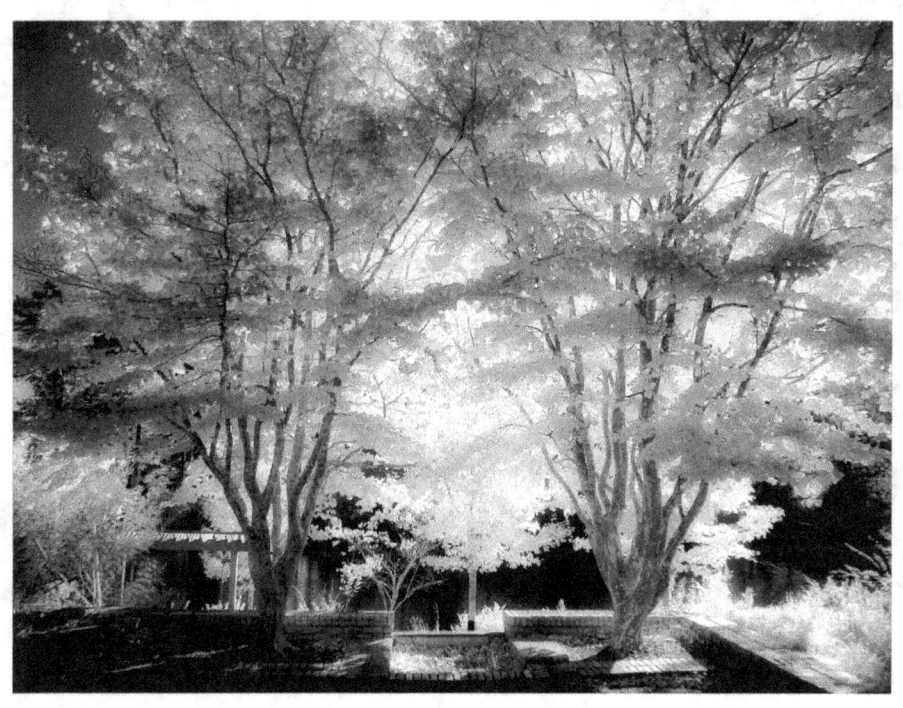

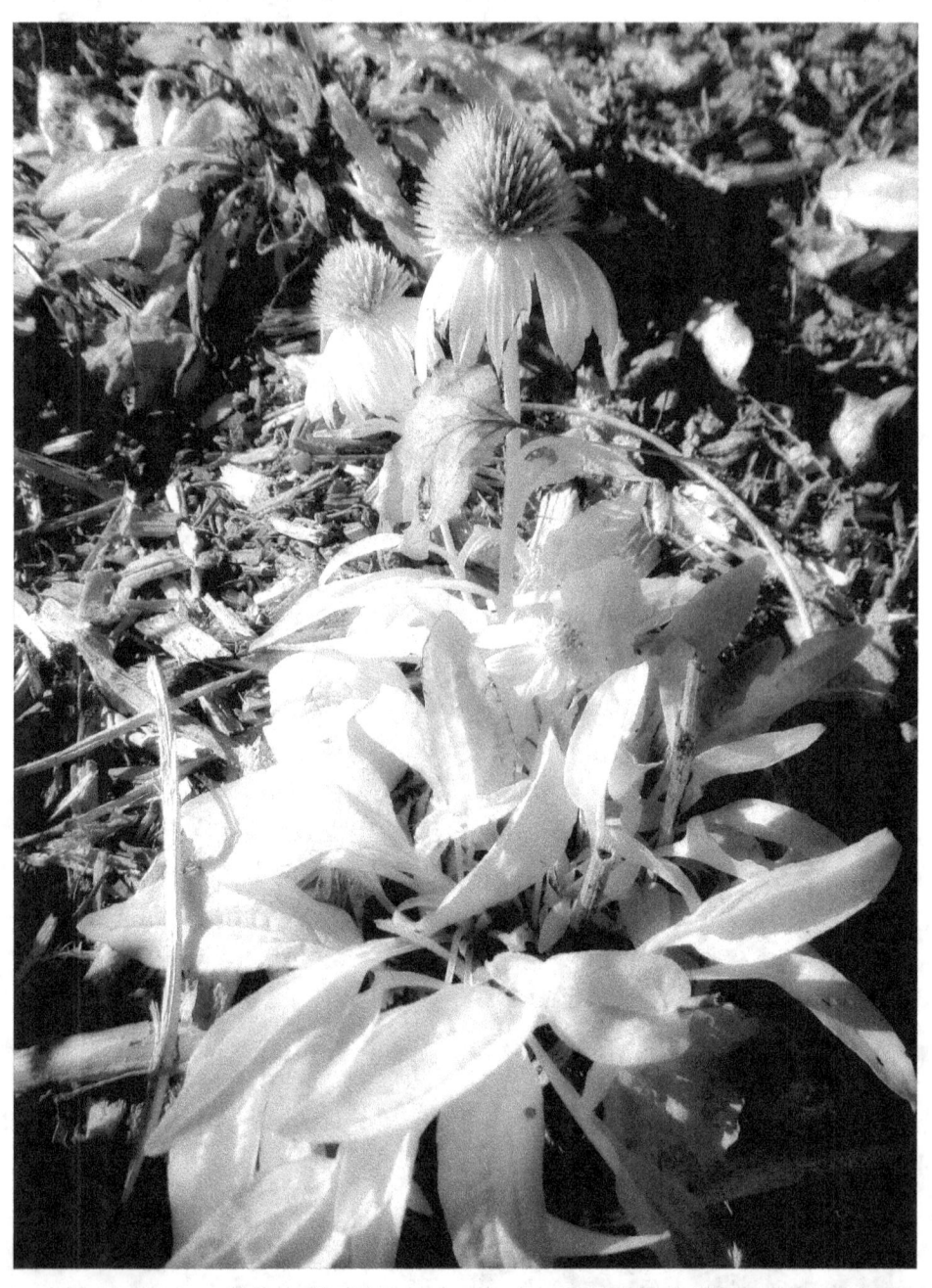

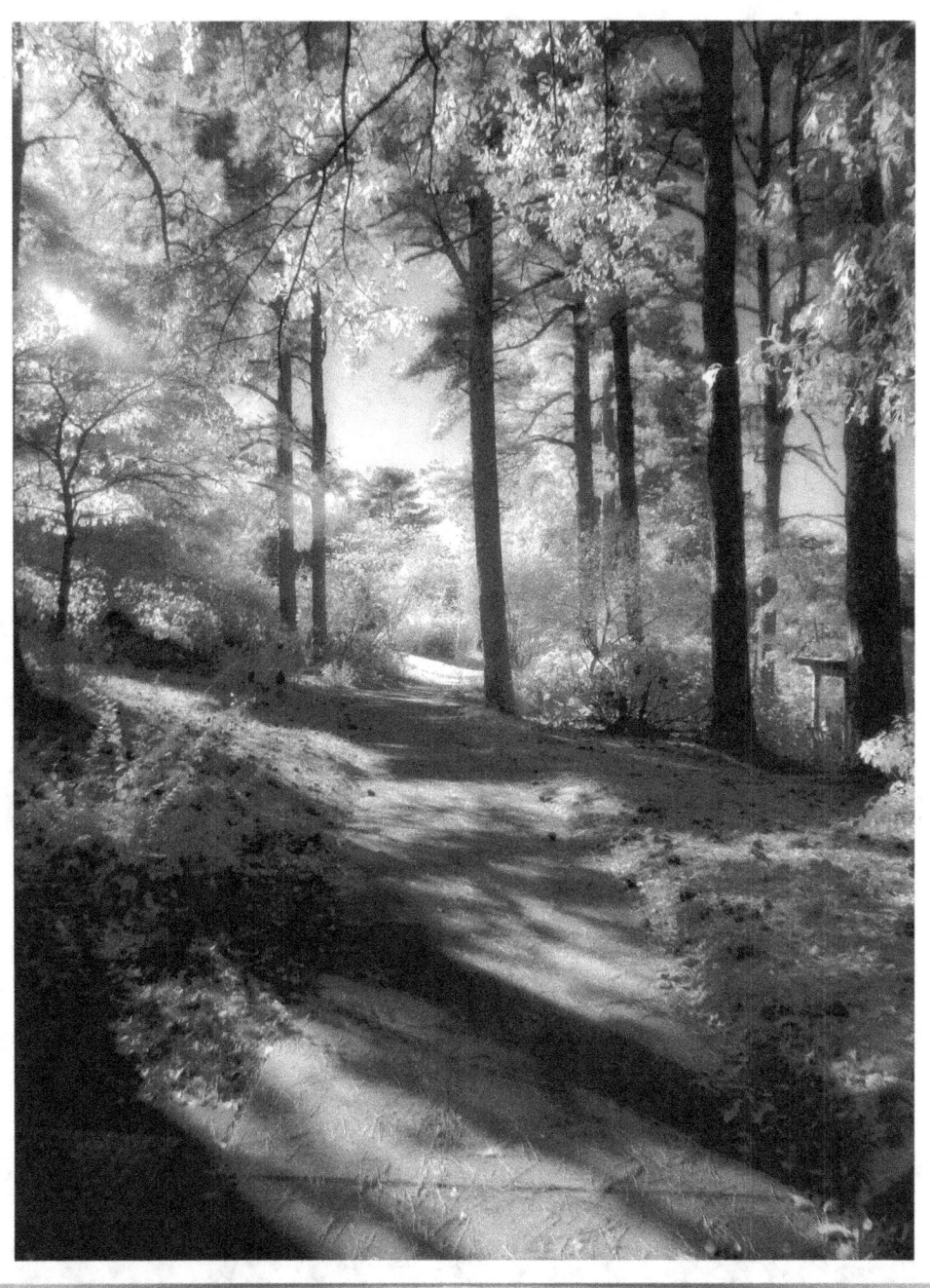

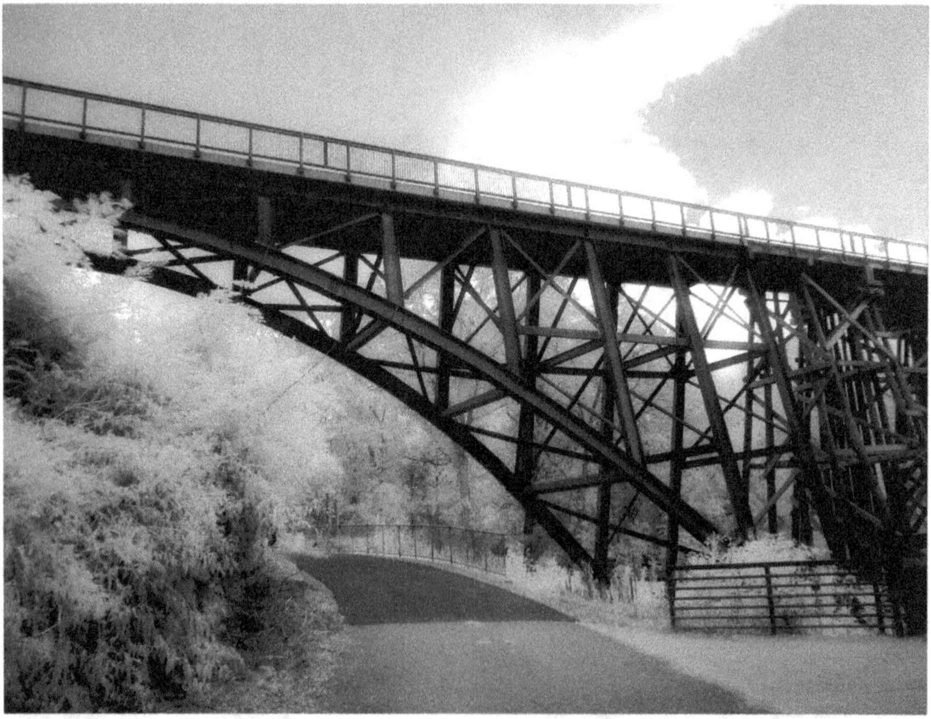

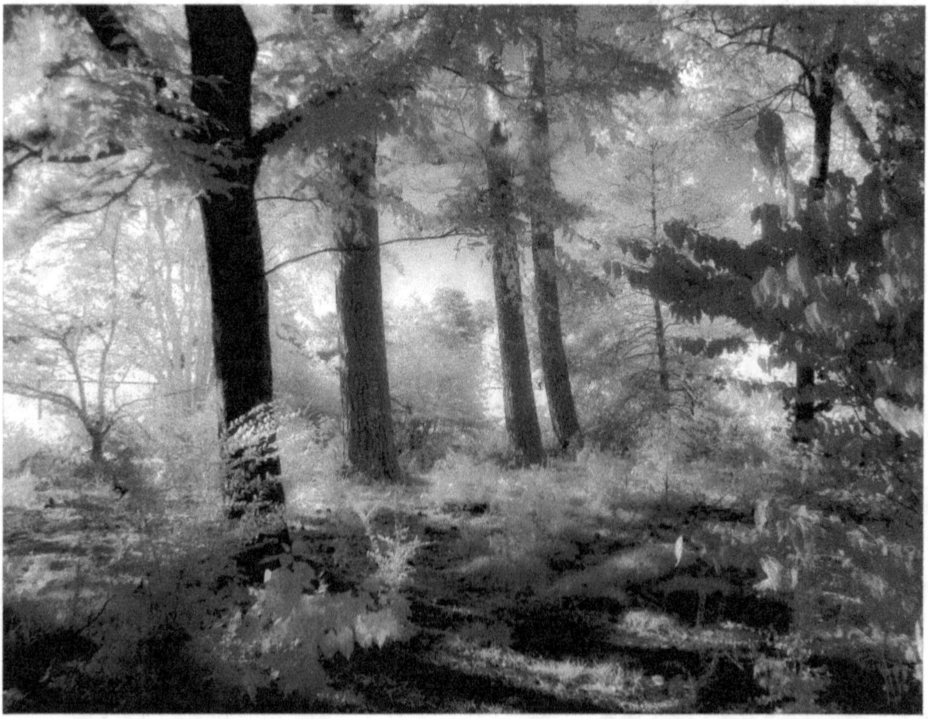

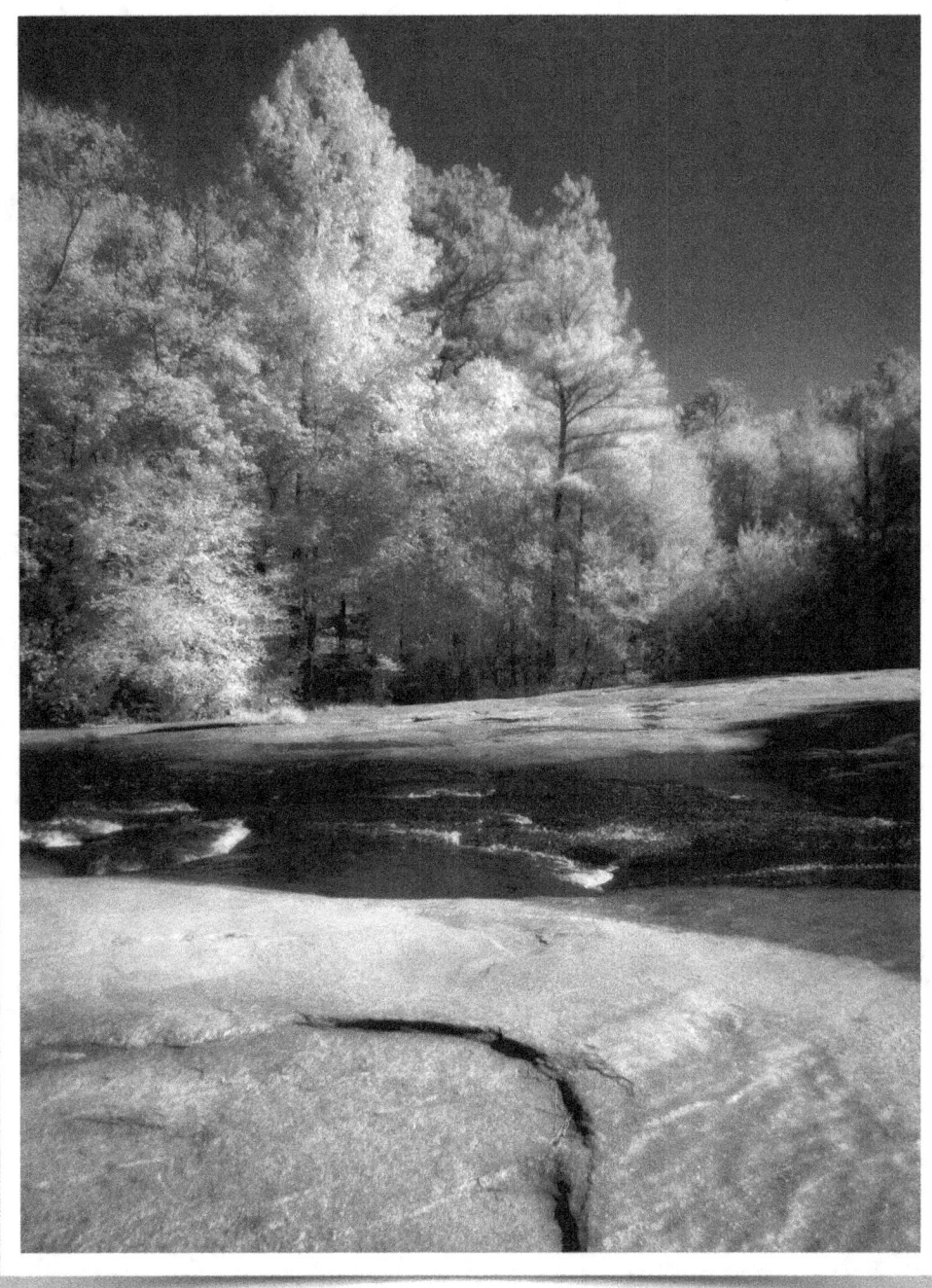

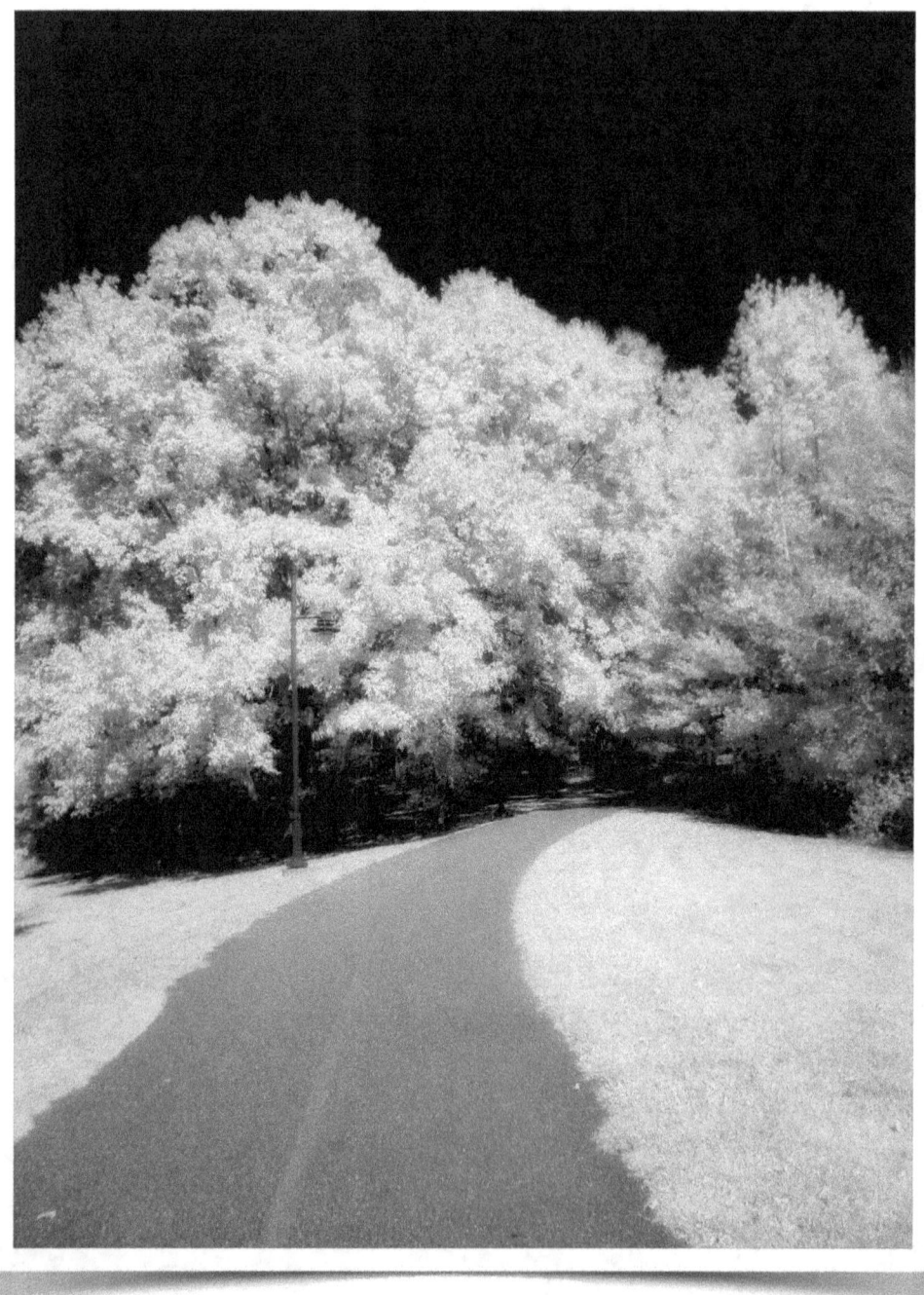

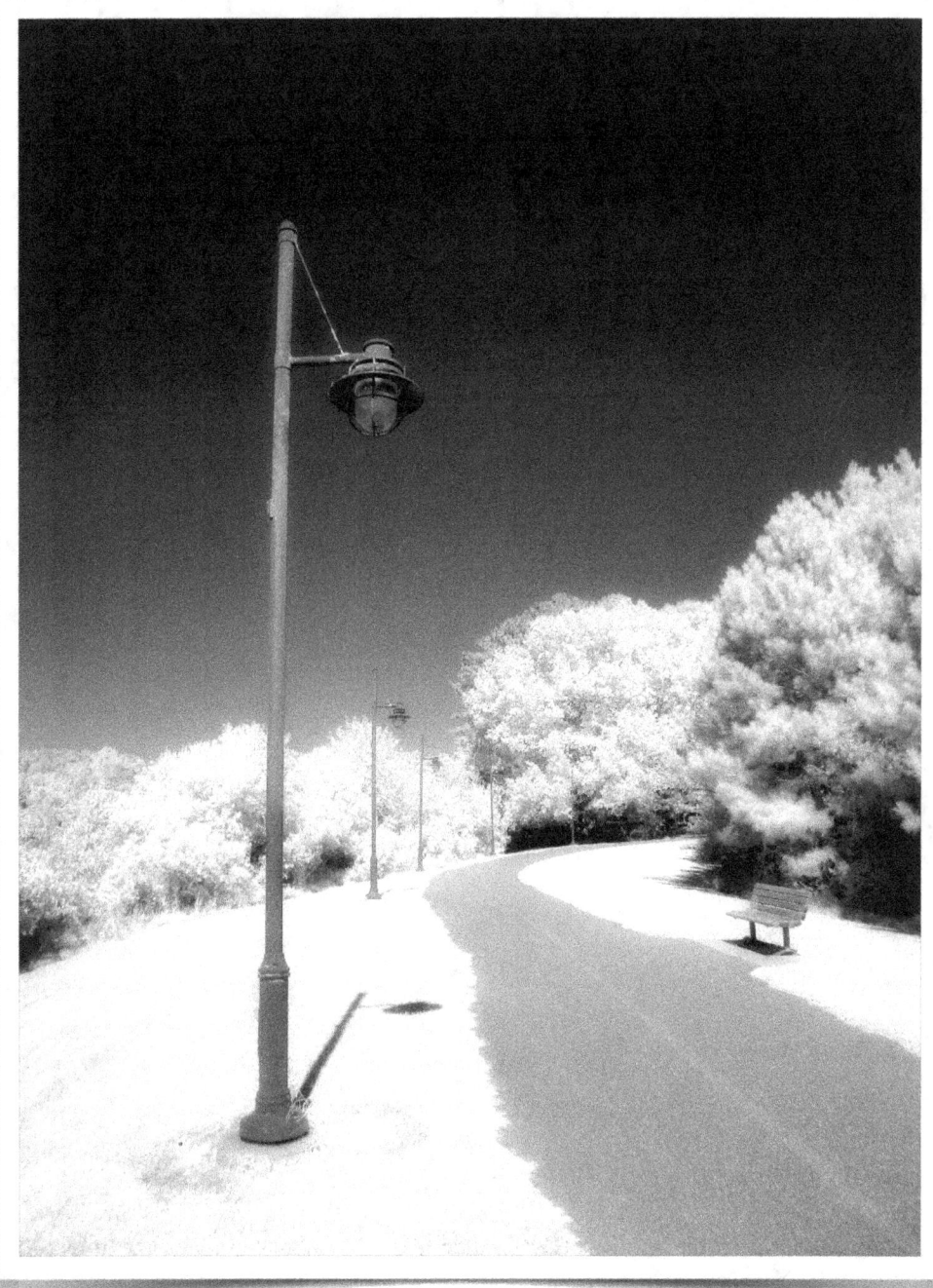

www.ingramcontent.com/pod-product-compliance
Lightning Source LLC
Chambersburg PA
CBHW030109230526
45471CB00003B/1338